I'm Just
Beginning to See

I'm Just Beginning to See
<u>A Story in the Songs of</u> Justin Hayward

A Revision — with an Introduction,
seven Conclusions, and a few Frames of Reference.

By
Adam Randolph

Broken Wing Books
Honolulu, Hawaii
Not For Profit

...and we shall find that the mind has no existence by itself; it is only the glitter of the sun on the surface of the waters.

—D. H. Lawrence

An Introduction

1. Seven LPs.

I'm Just Beginning to See is about the songs that Justin Hayward wrote for The Moody Blues from 1967 to 1972. The Moody Blues, who were Mike Pinder (mellotron), Ray Thomas (flute), Graeme Edge (drums), John Lodge (bass), Justin Hayward (guitar) and Tony Clarke (producer), made <u>seven</u> albums during those years that are, in the minds of most fans of The Moody Blues, very special. Among all the albums of music the band produced before and after, these seven LPs will always be set apart. And, for we who were young back then, they'll always be windows into the mysteries that were whirling around in our heads in the late 60's and early 70's .

The Seven LPs were:

1. Days of Future Passed (1967)
2. In Search of the Lost Chord (1968)
3. On the Threshold of a Dream (1969)
4. To Our Children's Children's Children (1969)
5. A Question of Balance (1970)
6. Every Good Boy Deserves Favour (1971)
7. Seventh Sojourn (1972)

The seven LPs were labeled concept albums — records with related songs and holding, more or less, to a single theme. One album was essentially about searching and another album was essentially about dreams. Each record had a beginning, a middle, and an end, and, if you listened to the lyrics and couldn't *see* a beginning, a middle, and an end, then it was up to the deeper recesses of your mind to *make* a beginning, a middle, and an end. The albums required the listener to create, for himself or herself, the narrative and images of the <u>stories</u> told. That, partly, was the charm of the albums. Along with the fact that it was very good music magnificently produced and realized.

There was a special fellowship among the band in those days — a true 'all for one and one for all' attitude. Certainly, there were no big egos wanting to stand out. All five wrote material for each of the seven albums and all five freely contributed to the production of the other members' songs. And, to enhance the fellowship and the wholeness of their albums, The Moody Blues overlapped their songs; the next song started before the previous song ended. Except, of course, for the two songs when you had to get up and turn the record over. But *that* little problem, for better or worse, has been taken care of now, hasn't it.

Graeme Edge, Ray Thomas, John Lodge, Mike Pinder, J. Hayward

8

2. The Premise.

So, seven Moody Blues albums with seven concepts. But *I'm Just Beginning to See* won't be about any of those seven concepts — not directly at least. *I'm Just Beginning to See* is going to be about a <u>secret concept</u> that's only in the songs Justin Hayward wrote, all of Justin Hayward's songs, on those seven albums — beginning with his first song on the first album, *Tuesday Afternoon* on *Days of Future Passed,* and ending with his last song on the seventh album, *The Land of Make Believe* on *Seventh Sojourn.*

The Premise of *I'm Just Beginning to See*

There is a story told in Justin Hayward's songs — a separate thread that runs through the seven LPs. You can think of it as Justin Hayward's own story or you can imagine Justin Hayward is telling a story that he invented. But in either event, it will be the story of a young man searching for truth. And there *will be* a beginning, a middle, and an end.

---

3. Mind You...

— Three of the songs in this story were co-written with Ray Thomas and one of the songs was co-written with Graeme Edge.

— Although they are not in the story, I am going to reference some of Justin Hayward's songs not on the seven LPs. Justin's story can be better explained and more clearly understood by citing these songs.

— *I'm Just Beginning to See* is not about Justin Hayward; there are no connections made between his life, of which I know little, and the story in the songs. This is 100% my take on Justin Hayward's songs.

4. The Internet and I.

I put a muddled version of *I'm Just Beginning to See* on the internet for a year or so back in 2005. But eventually, with a click, I removed it. It was just too incomplete and needed more work from me to recount more clearly the story that I'd seen in Justin Hayward's songs. (Also, back then, I ventured into the www internet world of The Moody Blues. For me, it was quite an experience — an unexpectedly rough and tumble territory.)

5. Kindred Books and Kindred Minds.

The ideas I came up with about Justin Hayward's songs weren't pulled out of my hat; I couldn't have told this story, or even have noticed it, without the context given in these books that had been collecting dust on my bookshelf.

My main references and inspirations were:

1. *Demian* by Hermann Hesse
2. *Jung and Hesse: a Record of Two Friendships* by Miguel Serrano
3. *The Teachings of Don Juan: a Yaqui Way of Knowledge* by Carlos Castaneda
4. *The Power of Myth* by Joseph Campbell
5. *Zen Bones and Zen Flesh* by Paul Reps
6. *In the Falcon's Claw: A Novel of the Year* 1000 by Chet Raymo
7. *Leaves of Grass* by Walt Whitman
8. *Reflections of Henry Miller* edited by Twinka Thiebaud
9. *The Tao of Pooh* by Benjamin Hoff
10. *David & the Phoenix* by Edward Ormandroyd
11. *On The Narrow Road* by Lesley Downer

These are the books that were piled on my table as I wrote *I'm Just Beginning to See.*

But there were others, as well, lingering in my head who each in their own way also helped me write this book. They were: the poets Sylvia Plath, Gerald Manley Hopkins and Arthur Rimbaud, the singer/songwriters Cat Stevens, Linda Lewis and Livingston Taylor, the painter Vincent Van Gogh, the naturalists Henry David Thoreau and John Muir, the cartoonist Walt Kelly, and the writers Lewis Carroll, Nikos Kazantzakis, and Antoine de Saint-Exupery. And one movie made of John Fowles' book, *The Magus.*

11

6. Me and this Book.

As for me, I am a self-exiled American English teacher in Okehazama, Japan.

In 2003, I quit my several jobs and set out to start my own English school with an idea to teach English the way I thought English should be taught. At which point I suddenly had the mother of all panic attacks — "I can't do this." But I had already burnt all my bridges. Somehow I ended up taking myself to Thailand; and there, in that land that reveres elephants, I started wandering around for weeks on end.

Eventually I ended up at the Chat Chai Hotel in Hua Hin, Thailand.

There, while sitting on the beach in the shade of the mountains behind me one evening, my mind knocked up against a favorite song of mine, *Tuesday Afternoon.* What *was* Justin Hayward "just beginning to see?" And the next evening, sitting in the same place, I thought about another song of Justin Hayward's. I thought about *Voices in the Sky* and the "bluebird flying high" and Justin asking it to "tell me what you sing." And I wondered *why* Justin Hayward wanted to know what the bluebird was singing about?

Then, the very next day, I was walking down a street in Hua Hin and I saw Hermann Hesse's *Demian* on a bookrack on the street in front of a shop. Justin Hayward's songs and now *Demian*. Why were these two big parts of my life many years in the past suddenly showing up in my head in 2003 in Thailand. Something, I figured, was telling me that I needed to re-explore the both of them again. So I started with *Demian*. I bought the book, went back to the Chat Chai Hotel, flopped on my bed and started to read, for the second time, *Demian: The Story of Emil Sinclair's Youth.*

This time I read it thoughtfully.

"But each of us — experiments of the depths — strives toward his own destiny. We can understand one another; but each of us is (only)*able to interpret himself to himself alone."*

—from the prologue of *Demian*

When I'd read *Demian* in 1970, the book had knocked me off my feet. And that's exactly what Justin Hayward's songs had done to me, too, in 1970 — knocked me off my feet. And in 1970, when I was 20 years old, I didn't have a clue about why Hermann Hesse's *Demian* and Justin Hayward's songs had so affected me.

13

It took me three afternoons to finish reading the book *Demian,* and all the time I was reading it, and understanding it more clearly, I was thinking about the songs of Justin Hayward. And over these three days I discovered a story in Justin Hayward's songs. First, my mind knocked up against the song *You Can Never Go Home.* Then, I began to see something in the word "anymore" in that song. And then, a door opened on <u>a story in the songs</u> of Justin Hayward — a story that would explain to me the spell the songs had held over me when I was young.

The next day I started writing *I'm Just Beginning to See* in my cheap, but very nice!, small room at the Chat Chai Hotel.

7. In a Nutshell.

As I was writing the story I had found in the songs of Justin Hayward, I wondered if anybody was ever going to understand what I was putting down on paper. I decided to try to sum the story all up in a nutshell, if I could, so that my Readers could get an idea of what would be in store for them in this short, little book *I'm Just Beginning to See.*

Maybe these words spoken by Justin Hayward introducing the song *The Other Side of Life* would best explain the story:

"Once upon a time a man went out in search of Enlightenment. And, he found himself. And he saw himself as he really was."

That's pretty good, but...

14

...then I stumbled on something a little better. It comes from the Native Americans. When I discovered it, I instantly knew that this was the exact outline of the story in the songs — from *Tuesday Afternoon* to *The Land of Make-Believe*:

"There comes a time in each of our lives when we are given the choice to follow a path that will take us deep within ourselves to discover the secrets of our own existence — to become a seeker. Should we decide to embark on this journey, we can never turn back. Our lives are changed forever. The true seeker will walk alone through dense forests and hot deserts. It takes stamina and endurance to walk this path and the terrain is often narrow and rocky. On this journey there are many places for them to slip into and hide. And the faces of deceit and of sadness and of darkness await them everywhere. But the path goes on. The true seeker stays the course, wounded at times, exhausted and out of energy. Many times he will struggle back to his feet, to take only a few more steps, before falling again. Rested, he forges on, continuing the treacherous path. One day the battle and the loneliness and the desperate fights are over and the sun breaks through the clouds. The battle of the dark night of the soul is won. A new path is now laid before them. A gentler path filled with a new awareness. Now, though they are not permitted to walk the path for others, they *can* love and guide and be a living example of the truth."

A Reading Suggestion or Two and...

First, you should keep the words "I'm looking at myself, reflections of my mind" in *your* mind as you read through *I'm Just Beginning to See;* they really do tell us what Justin Hayward is doing in his songs on the seven LPs.

Also, I think that reading lyrics and then reading a lit major explain the lyrics as he sees them could be a little boring – so I've tried to make this as short and to the point as I can. If you are a true fan of Justin Hayward, just take a deep breath, relax, turn your concentration up just a little, and before you know it you'll be through to the end.

The ideas that I have about the songs may at times seem to be heading in different directions but, if you will just allow me a little <u>poetic</u> <u>license</u> (especially regarding "the Compadre") throughout this trip, I think you'll find they all come together in the end.

All I can hope is that *I'm Just Beginning to See* might give the Reader some intuitive insight into Justin Hayward's amazing songs.

...a Thank You
to Masako, Pete and John.

17

Justin Hayward, Back Then.

I'm Just Beginning to See

A Prologue

The Music of Heaven

An Ancient Story of Tao and of String Theory.

Over five thousand years ago two Chinese men, one old and one young, are sitting by a river. The Old Man, the teacher, says to the Young Man, his student, "there is the music of People and the music of the Earth and the Music of Heaven." The Young Man thinks for a bit and then says, "I know the music of People. I hear it when beautiful Li Ching plays her Flute. And it is very nice. And I know the music of the Earth. I can hear it when the Wind blows through the Trees. And it, too, is very nice. But what is the Music of Heaven?" The Old Man simply answers, "What do you suppose is behind it all?"

Shush ... and you will
have your beginning.
—Linda Lewis, *Lark*

The First LP — Days of Future Passed

In which voices are heard and a lonely journey is begun.

Song One — Tuesday Afternoon
(The Forever Afternoon)

Here is my secret. It's very simple:
One <u>sees</u> well only with the heart.
The essential is invisible to the eyes.
—The Fox in *The Little Prince*

OK. Here we go.

Tuesday Afternoon
I'm just beginning to see
Now I'm on my way.
It doesn't matter to me
Chasing the clouds away.

It's a Tuesday afternoon and Justin is just getting a glimmer of something that ... might be meaningful. But what is it? And a happy, carefree journey someplace is just starting. But to where?

Something calls to me
The trees are drawing me near
I've got to find out why
Those gentle voices I hear
Explain it all with a sigh.

But this isn't just *any* Tuesday afternoon. It's the forever afternoon — the forever afternoon when a strange adventure begins. Something very powerful is happening inside Justin; a mysterious connection between Justin and Nature itself is beginning. And it's this fantastic communication with the "gentle voices" that's going to impel Justin to be "on his way."

Hermann Hesse wrote in *Demian*: "To surrender to Nature's irrational, strangely confused formations produces in us a feeling of inner harmony with the forces responsible for these phenomena. We soon fall prey to the temptation of thinking of them as being our own moods, our own creations, and see the boundaries separating us from Nature quiver and dissolve..."

And, in the bouncy part of the song, that's exactly what Justin does do — surrender to Nature.

I'm looking at myself
Reflections of my mind
It's just the kind of day
To leave myself behind.

Is what Justin's seeing on the surface of his retina coming from outside or coming from inside? Is what Justin's hearing on the surface of his eardrums coming from outside or coming from inside?

And why in the world is Justin "leaving himself behind?" Isn't taking yourself along on a journey important? No matter *where* you're going. Then again, maybe there's a *reason* Justin's leaving himself behind.

24

Could this reason be found in what Henry Miller said? Could it be that: "Until we lose ourselves there is no hope of ever finding ourselves?" It's a paradoxical idea, but, yes, Justin *is* doing exactly that that he has to do — to "find out why," he's got to "lose his way" and "go completely astray." (JH's *The Other Side of Life*)

So gently swaying through
The fairyland of love.
If you'll just come with me
You'll see the beauty of
Tuesday afternoon.

In any event, all the beauty of the forever afternoon and all of the sounds of the forever afternoon have started Justin on a journey.

("I knew who I was this morning but I've changed a few times since then," said Alice.)

And though these ad-ventures are always set out on alone, Justin's been kind enough to invite us along, hasn't he. You re-member, don't you? "If you'll just come with me/ You'll see the beauty of/ Tuesday Afternoon."

OK, Justin, since it's all the same to you then, we'll be tagging along.

25

Song Two — Nights in White Satin

The path does not start with light and
ecstasy; it starts with hard tacks and pain,
and with disappointment and confusion.
—the Buddha

The story that begins with *Tuesday Afternoon* and ends with *The Land of Make Believe* mostly takes place in Justin's heart and head. But that's not where the story is now. In *Nights in White Satin* Justin's coping with things in the real world.

Nights in white satin
Never reaching the end.
Letters I've written
Never meaning to send.

"Sleepless are the hours / And lonely is the night / For the poor tormented soul / Who is searching for the light." Justin Hayward sings these words in the song *This Morning* (from *Blue Jays* with John Lodge) to describe the "pain" and "confusion" that the young truth seeker experiences on the early days of the path.

Beauty I'd always missed
With these eyes before.
Just what the truth is
I can't say any more.

This sounds like John Keats, doesn't it? "'Beauty is truth, truth beauty,' — that is all/Ye know on earth, and all ye need to know." But, for Justin, any truth that was discovered in *Tuesday Afternoon* is now missing here in *Nights in White Satin*.

'Cos I love you/Yes I love you/Oh how I love you.

And so there's something else on Justin's mind as he starts out on the path — he's in love. A little complication that he'll just have to deal with as best he can.

Gazing at people
Some hand in hand.
Just what I'm going through
They can't understand.

Imagining there's a mark on his forehead that has somehow separated him from the rest of humanity, Justin walks the desolate streets of the night.

Some try to tell me
Thoughts they cannot defend.

Maybe it was someone pushing her religion at the door or maybe it was some Hare Krishna dancers on the street selling nirvana. For Justin, though, their "thoughts," their truths, don't make any sense and he just can't buy whatever it is they're selling. "Deceit kills the Light," sang Cat Stevens.

And then, in these last two lines of *Nights in White Satin*, <u>Fate</u> steps into the story in the songs:

Just what you want to be
You will be in the end.

In the stillness of the dark, early morning hours Justin perceives that a destiny has joined him on this new and disorienting detour that he's found himself on. And the deeply emotional experience of it, this realization of Fate, sparks an understanding of a different interpretation of reality; and it leaves Justin with no other choice but to follow the 'difficult path.' The path that leads to the world within.

The future enters into us,
In order to transform itself in us,
Long before it happens.
—Rainer Maria Rilke

Second LP — In Search of the Lost Chord

In which the true source of the gentle voices heard
is discovered.

Song Three — Voices in the Sky

I admit, I desire,
Occasionally, some backtalk
From the mute sky.
—Sylvia Plath
  Black Rook in Rainy Weather

Justin's "on his way" but on his way to where? And
which way to head?

Looking round, Justin doesn't see a signpost point-
ing to the road he should take; nor is there anything
lying about labeled <u>eat me</u> or <u>drink me</u>, either.

In *Voices in the Sky* Justin decides to ask around
for directions.

Bluebird flying high
Tell me what you sing.
If you could talk to me
What news would you bring
Of voices in the sky.

And it's Nature Justin turns to first; and he starts
with the sky and the birds that travel there. They'll
know something. They can see for miles. They'll
certainly have a clue or two. Won't they?

Nightingale hovering high
Harmonize the wind.
Darkness your symphony
I can hear you sing
Of voices in the sky.

Justin's expecting an answer from the Sky that will tell him the way to go—but the Bluebird and the Nightingale and even the chirring insects can't help him.

Just what is happening to me
I lie awake with the sound of the sea
Calling to me.

In *Nights in White Satin* Justin sang, "Just what I'm going through/<u>They</u> can't understand." In *Voices in the Sky* Justin's *now* singing, "Just what is happening to me," <u>I</u> can't understand.
That's not any progress at all, is it?

Old man passing by
Tell me what you sing.
Though your voice be faint
I am listening.
Voices in the sky.

Children with the skipping rope
Tell me what you sing.
Playtime is nearly gone
The bell's about to ring./Voices in the sky.

31

People old and young; the wisdom of many years and the innocence of only a few years. No. Nothing there. Nada.

But, maybe, the road that Justin's looking for isn't an actual road in the actual world. Maybe the road that he needs to take is somewhere inside himself.

Song Four — Visions of Paradise
co-written with Ray Thomas

I swear to you there are divine things
more beautiful than words can tell.
—Walt Whitman

Visions of Paradise begins with Ray Thomas's flute taking us someplace deep inside. There's just no doubt about it, is there. We *are* going deep — into the Intuitive, into the Transcendental.

We're now going to take a fantastic voyage inside; we're going to start taking a good look at things inside — to see ourselves as we really are.

The great expert on "things inside," the unconscious, was Carl Jung, a psychiatrist back in the days when there weren't psychiatrists and psychologists on every other block. In the early 1900's, at the same time that astronomers were discovering the unfathomable size of our star filled universe, Carl Jung was discovering the unfathomable size of our inner universe, the unconscious. There are, then, *two* universes. And, it is in between the two universes that we live our lives.

Carl Jung discovered the Anima—the goddess aspect of our unconscious. And the seeker meets her not long after he sets out. This fantastic encounter with the Anima becomes, in fact, the essence of Justin's whole endeavor on the path. And, as he goes deeper and deeper in *Visions of Paradise*, he'll meet, first, Eve (desire) then second, Helen (insight) then third, Mary (virtue) and then fourth, Sophia (truth).

According to Joseph Campbell, in *The Power of Myth*, the most important thing learned from the goddess(es) "down, down, down" is "a compassion for all living things." I like the word, kindness.

33

Justin will "reflect" on the encounter with *his* goddess throughout his journey on the path; it will always be a thing ... more "beautiful than word can tell."

The sounds in my mind
Just come to me,
Come see, come see.
And the call of her eyes
Makes waterfalls,
Of me, of me.

In this first verse of the song we're invited to "come see" the "sounds" in Justin's mind. Strange, but <u>inside</u>, fantastic things *are* possible.
And the "call of her eyes."
The goddess's eyes — they're making waterfalls of Justin. He really is in some kind of Wonderland.

In the garden of her love
I'll stay awhile,
To be, to be.

In the goddess's garden of love Justin "stays awhile." And *there* something happens. And what does happen there has to do with Justin's Fate.

What the seeds of her thoughts
Wants me to be,
Come see, come see.

The seeds of Justin's Fate, what the goddess wants him to be, are in the ground. And what seeds are destined to become, they will become.

And then there's Ray Thomas's flute again. Deeper and *even deeper* Justin goes.

Visions of paradise
Cloudless skies I see.
Rainbows on the hill
Blue onyx on the sea
Come see, Come see.

The sky and the rainbow and the blue onyx on the sea are all kaleidoscoping in Justin's head — and Justin's reeling in an ether *beyond* beauty.

Here is the efflux of the soul.
    —Walt Whitman

35

Song Five — The Actor

Fear is like a giant fog. It sits on your
brain and blocks everything — real
feelings, true happiness, real joy. They
can't get through that fog. But you lift it,
buddy, you're in for the ride of your life.
    —Albert Brooks in the
      movie *Defending Your Life*

Justin is finding life in the real world, the traffic and
the telephones, a little rough these days. There's too
much going on inside his head. In *The Actor* he's
feeling just like an actor — literally performing the daily
duties of life. Because all the while he's dealing with
what's happening in the real world — *outside* — he's
also dealing with what's happening in the fantastic
world — *inside.*

The curtain rises on the scene
With someone chanting to be free.
The play unfolds before my eyes
There stands the actor who is me./(verse)
The sleeping hours take us far
From traffic, telephones and fear.
Put out your problems with the cat
Escape until a bell you hear.

Justin is confronting Fear now and his only respite from this Fear is sleep. Or so he thinks. The unavoidable truth is that all the faces inside must be met; and escape is not the answer. The Yaqui desert-walker Don Juan, said: "When a man starts to learn, he is never clear about his objectives. He slowly begins to learn — bit by bit at first, then in big chunks. And his thoughts soon clash. What he learns is never what he pictured, and so he begins to be afraid. And the fear begins to mount mercilessly. And thus he has stumbled upon the first of his natural enemies: Fear!"

But in Justin's life, in the *real* world, there's also a *real* girl that he's in love with. Is he acting for her, too?

Our reasons are the same
But there's no one we can blame
For there's nowhere we need go
And the only truth we know comes so easily.
The sound I have heard in your hello
Oh darling, you're almost part of me
Oh darling, you're all I'll ever see.

37

The "only truth we know" — an eternal truth — two young people in love. It's not a complicated thing. Nor is it a thing that can be helped — for "there's no one we can blame."

Next, *The Actor*'s two <u>rainy afternoon verses</u>. Two young people in their two separate rooms — two young hearts coping with love and life and with the Mystery and all its questions. The "actors" here are, of course, Justin and the girl he loves.

It's such a rainy afternoon,
No point in going anywhere.
The sounds just drift across my room
I wish this feeling I could share.

It's such a rainy afternoon
She sits and gazes from her window.
Her mind tries to recall his face
A feeling deep inside her grows.

Are the paths taken by men and women different? Carl Jung thought so: "Women are increasingly aware that Love alone can give them full stature, just as men are beginning to divine that only the spirit can give life its highest meaning. Both seek a psychic relationship, because Love needs the spirit, and the spirit Love, for its completion." Men seeking themselves on paths and woman seeking themselves through the men *on* those paths. (It's somehow like that book I never read: *Why Men Don't Listen and Women Don't Read Maps.*)

A Break — The Land of No-Words

This is thy hour O soul,
thy free flight into the wordless.
—Walt Whitman

We need to take a break for a moment and think about the unconscious — the Land of No-Words. The location of this story.

Down, down, down,
Where your dreams are found.
They're sleeping inside of us all.

These three lines, from Justin Hayward's song *Nights, Winters, Years* on *Blue Jays,* can send shivers through me.

39

And who *are* "they" that are "sleeping inside of us all?"

"They" are not only the Goddess that Justin met in *Visions of Paradise,* but "they" are also the "faces of deceit and of sadness and of darkness" that Justin is now just starting to deal with. And there will be others "inside," as well. And what will they have to say to Justin? Nothing. And they never will have a word to say. Because the unconscious is the land of no-words; and all the lessons learned there, inside where our "dreams are found," are learned in a world that is without words.

A man whose name is unknown to me wrote this: "The land of words and the land of no-words don't comprehend each other — words must stop at the frontier of no-words. It is foolish to throw words at the land of no-words — all it can do is mislead."

(Yes. But words are all the Poets have!)

So, it is in this land of no-words, the unconscious, where most this story in the songs takes place. And it is in *this* land that the seeker treks. And it is in *this* land that, one by one and step by step, the seeker encounters all that he or she must encounter — "they" that are "sleeping inside of us all."

Third LP — On the Threshold of a Dream

In which not only a new friend but also a dark and frightening presence is found.

Song Six — Lovely to See You

Two Drifters
Off to see the world.
—Johnny Mercer

In *Lovely to See You* we meet the Compadre.

The Compadre, Justin's strange, newfound travelling companion, might be mistaken for the inner voice. But that's not the case. The Compadre's something altogether different. To me, the Compadre's a steady and true confederate sent out from the land of no-words, the unconscious, to be with Justin as he makes his way along the path — and an avatar of all that is inside. And, in spite of being from the land of no-words, 'words' *work* between Justin and the Compadre. Which is very comforting for anyone who's travelling the long and lonely road within.

Lovely to see You starts with Justin finding the Compadre right there on his doorstep.

Wonderful day for passing my way
Knock on my door and even the score
With your eyes
Lovely to see you again my friend
Walk along with me to the next bend.

The Compadre

Justin's I'm-at-a-disadvantage feelings on this path endeavor are now gone; the Compadre has "evened the score." There's a new found purchase in Justin's step and he has a new *huckleberry friend* — and they're *after the same rainbow's end.*

And then, in the next verse of the song, Justin can, with the new strength that the Compadre's arrival has given him, start working through the fear that he sang about in *The Actor.*

Dark cloud of fear is blowing away
Now that you're here, you're going to stay,
'Cos it's lovely to see you again my friend.

Next, out of the Blue!, something entirely new. Justin starts time-travelling. But *this* time-travelling is all going to take place in Justin's own head.

Tell us what you've seen
In faraway forgotten lands
Where empires have turned back to sand.

How interesting! What could this time-travelling business be all about? Has the Compadre actually *seen* these "faraway forgotten lands," that are now in ruins, that have "turned back to sand?"

It's all getting "curiouser and curiouser" and the world inside now seems *wider than a mile.*

43

Song Seven — Never Comes the Day

Let my heart be still a moment
and this mystery explore.
—Edgar Allen Poe

In *Visions of Paradise* we met the Goddess. In *Never Comes the Day* we meet the Darkness — the ever-present dark brother or sister in all of us. This Darkness, that Hermann Hesse described in *Demian* as a "forbidden stream that roars beneath the surface," is neither a dragon to be slain nor a beast to be defeated. It is a natural, instinctive and irrational part of us that's encountered by all seekers. And all the seeker needs to do, to deal with this Darkness, is just understand it.

*If you bring forth what is within you,
What you bring forth will save you.*
— Jesus

Because the seeker's duty is to see himself as he *really* is. And, so, once he knows and acknowledges the Darkness inside, he won't ever have to fear the Darkness again.

But the discovery of this Darkness is unnerving. And, in the song *Never Comes the Day,* Justin *does* think that he's been possessed by a shadowy dæmon of a sort. And he wonders if his friends and his lover, as well, can *see* this shadowy dæmon inside him.

Work away today, think about tomorrow
Never comes the day for my love and me.
I feel her gently sighing as the evening slips away.
<u>If only you knew what's inside of me now</u>
<u>You wouldn't want to know me somehow.</u>

Does the beautiful girl that Justin loves so much, lying next to him, does she see this Darkness inside him? Isn't it there in his face for all to see?

Justin's thoughts are scattered and the rest of the song is sung not only to her but, also, to himself and to the Compadre, as well.

To Her:

But you will love me tonight
We alone will be alright/In the end.

Justin thinks that someday, "in the end," all that he's "going through" will be over and that he and the girl he loves will find happiness together.

Give just a little bit more
Take a little bit less/From each other tonight.

To Himself:

Admit what you're feeling
And see what's in front of you
It's never out of your sight.
You know it's true.

What's never "out of" Justin's "sight" is the still unclear idea of Enlightenment.

And, to the Compadre:

We all know that it's true.

Song Eight — Are You Sitting Comfortably
co-written with Ray Thomas

Myth illuminates the
obscurity of the Creator.
—Carl Jung

Are You Sitting Comfortably is the Myth Song.
The myths of antiquity, that all the original cultures that ever existed on Earth created, were stories that helped us, as Bill Moyers said in his conversation with Joseph Campbell on PBS's *The Power of Myth*, "touch the eternal, understand the mysterious and find out who we are."
So why are the myths showing up here in Justin's story? They're here because all the symbolic truths *of*

the myths, all wordless by nature, *are* in our heads. Carl Jung discovered in us the <u>collective unconscious</u>. This collective unconscious, which is inherited (it's in our very DNA), carries within it 'secrets' from the past. And it is via this inherited part of our unconscious minds, identical in all of us, that we can actually go back in time, in our own heads, and retrieve ancient knowledge not only of the myths but, also, even more ancient knowledge of the time *before* the myths.

Take another sip my love
And see what you will see
A fleet of golden galleons,
On a crystal sea.
Are you sitting comfortably?
Let Merlin cast his spell.

Ride along the winds of time
And see where we have been.
The glorious age of Camelot
When Guinevere was Queen.
 It all unfolds before your eyes
As Merlin casts his spell.

The seven wonders of the world
He'll lay before your feet
In far-off lands, on distant shores,
So many friends to meet.
Are you sitting comfortably?
Let Merlin cast his spell.

Camelot and Guinevere and Merlin. The myth of heroes and the myth of maidens and the myth of magic. And "so many friends to meet."

One friend could be the Japanese Moon Princess Orihimè who meets her lover along the Milky Way on the 7th day of the 7th month of every year. Or yet another friend could be Silap Inua who minds the cold sky and the cold wind for the Eskimo. And then there's David's good friend — the one and only Phoenix.

There were *thousands and thousands* of them — *everywhere* — the dramatis personae of the myths. And in their stories heroes, not unlike the Justin in *this* story, "venture into regions of 'supernatural wonder' to encounter the strange powers and events there."

Tinirau of Polynesia — who protected the Oceans.

Fourth LP — To Our Children's Children's Children

In which an ancient kindred spirit is visited and the path is lost.

Song Nine — Gypsy

The soul that rises in us,
Our life's star,
Hath had elsewhere, its setting.
—Wm. Wordsworth

In *Gypsy,* Justin continues time-travelling within and goes back to a time before there even *were* myths. Back to a primitive time. Back to a primitive man. Back to the first man to wonder. The first man to seek.

The Gypsy.

And what has Justin discovered in the heart of the Gypsy? Panic and fear and many questions: Where did I come from? What *is* this land and this sky? What will become of me?

("A long time ago, back in the mists of time, back when the crystal waters flowed. There was a world...")

A Gypsy of a strange and distant time
Travelling in panic all directions blind.
Aching for the warmth of a burning sun
Freezing in the emptiness of where he'd come from.
Left without a hope of coming home.

49

Justin thinks, at this point on his journey along the path, that anyone "left without a hope of coming home" is tragically forsaken. But "home" is more than a place we left when we started out on our individual paths in life. Home is also an important aspect of the unconscious — and an aspect that Justin will splendidly deal with later on in this story in the songs.

Speeding through a shadow of a million years
Darkness is the only sound to reach his ears;
Frightening him with visions of eternity;
Screaming for a future that could never be.
Left without a hope of coming home.

Not long ago the Gypsy, a primitive man, was just one of the many creatures of the Earth. But now Man has left the other creatures and set out on his own new course. And on this new track he will have to face things that no other living and breathing being of the Earth has ever had to face before — his own soul and his own mortality.

And he is harrowed by this new challenge — through and through.

Song Ten — I Never Thought I'd Live to be a Hundred and I Never Thought I'd Live to be a Million

> I had reached the point that
> I had always wanted to reach,
> which was a complete step
> across chronological time
> into the timeless shadows.
> —Jack Kerouac *On the Road*

I Never Thought I'd Live to be a Hundred/a Million are two short songs about Man's spiritual struggle over the span of his time on Earth.

In *Hundred,* Man is young — just recently having opened his eyes to himself and to the circumstances of his own existence. In *Million,* Man is where he is today.

Hundred:

I never thought I'd live to be a hundred
I never thought I'd get to do the things
That all those other sons do, and they do.

I never thought I'd ever have my freedom
An age ago my maker was refusing me
The pleasure of the view.

An "age ago" was the time before Man's awakening. But "the pleasure of the view" that Man's awakening has brought, we shouldn't forget, has also brought the panic and the fear and the questions.

Million:

I never thought I'd get to be a million
I never thought I'd get to be the thing that
All his other children see. Look at me.

Man today. It's the "man today" circumstance that Justin is now working out for himself.

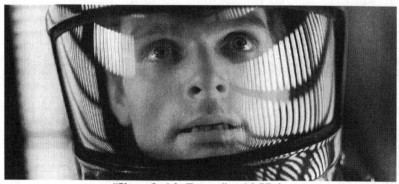

"I'm afraid, Dave," said Hal.

And one more thing about both of these songs. When Justin sings "all those other sons do" on *Hundred* and "all his other children see" on *Million,* I can't help but think about the movie *2001: A Space Odyssey.* I imagine other planets and I imagine other <u>men</u> and I imagine *their* hearts waking up to *their* own existence in *our* universe.

In any event, Justin's time-travelling is now over and he has brought himself back to the present.

<u>Song Eleven — Watching and Waiting</u>
co-written with Ray Thomas

And by and by Christopher Robin
came to an end of things, and he was
silent, and he sat there, looking out
over the world.
—from *Winnie the Pooh* by A. A. Milne

On *Watching and Waiting* Justin, now a little worn
out, finds himself on another beautiful *Tuesday After-
noon.* But *this* Tuesday Afternoon is not as enchanting
as the first one was — the forever afternoon. On *this*
Tuesday Afternoon Justin's very discouraged.

There, by the side of the path, against a great 1,000
year old tree, sits Justin — and he's lost.

Watching and waiting
For a friend to play with
Why have I been alone so long?

Justin, a lost and lonely seeker, doesn't realize the
progress that he's already made. He is, in fact, thinking
he's made no progress at all. He might even be
thinking that there never *was* a path.

Mole he is burrowing
His way to the sunlight
He knows there's someone there so strong.

53

The Mole, who lives its whole life underground, where the Light never shines, where even the song of the Bluebird can't be heard, *he's* making progress. The Mole's digging his way up to the sunlight. But not Justin. All Justin can do is sit there and watch and wait.

And so, on this <u>second</u> *Tuesday Afternoon*, the Gentle Voices of nature do their best to get Justin back on his way again.

'Cos here there's lots of room for doing
The things you've always been denied.
So, look and gather all you want to
There's no one here to stop you trying.

Only Nature will set you free and only Nature has all you'll ever need. But the words, these *pleas*, have no effect on Justin now.

And then, another voice is heard — a special voice. And it whispers this to Justin:

Soon you will see me,
'Cos I'll be all around you
But where I come from, I can't tell.

It's Justin's Fate. Always there.
And those words! "But where I come from, I can't tell." To me, they might be the most powerful words in the entire story in the songs. The words hit you in

the solar plexus and leave you breathless — they are perfect, exquisite mystery.

Then, the Gentle Voices continue to encourage and to hearten Justin — trying to get him back on the path and on his way again.

But don't be alarmed
By my fields and my forests
They're here for only you to share.

Justin though, sitting against the great 1,000 year old tree alongside the path, is lost and lonely and, now, a little impatient.

Watching and waiting
For someone to understand me
I hope it won't be very long.

Fifth LP — A Question of Balance
In which the lost path is discovered again.

<u>Question</u>: The song *Question* is two songs. Let's call the opening and closing parts *Question* and let's call the song sandwiched between the two parts of *Question The Middle Song.* (The song *Question* is a short, meaningful excursion on Justin's journey.)

<u>Song Twelve</u> — Question

Even though you can't expect to
defeat the absurdity of the world,
you must make the attempt.
   —Phil Ochs

Question is a loud shout at the powers of the world from the powerless of the world. "Please stop! You're destroying all the forever afternoons for all of us. You're destroying them with your businesses that count money more important than the life of a river, with your armies, every one of them with God on their side, with your politicians that trick and deceive those who trust them to do the right thing, and with your ideologies that lead their followers and their non-followers alike over high cliffs."

Why do we never get an answer
When we're knocking at the door
With a thousand million questions

About hate and death and war?
'Cos when we stop and look around us
There is nothing that we need
In a world of persecution
That is burning in its greed.
Why do we never get an answer
When we're knocking at the door
Because the truth is hard to swallow
That's what the war of love is for.

The "war" we thought we were fighting back then, somehow, ran out of steam. It seemed like one day it was there and then the next day it wasn't there. The Moody Blues finished their Seven LPs, (I went back to school), the top of the pops songs were now either disco's "we don't care about anything" or punk's "we *won't* care about anything" and Phil Ochs, who saw that it was all over and who had worked so hard in "the war of love," just left the scene entirely.

57

Song Thirteen — The Middle Song

My soul is lost, my friend.
Tell me, how do I begin again.
—Bruce Springsteen

In *The Middle Song* Justin's 100% lost — and 99% pessimistic about ever getting any place on his journey. He's not "on his way" anywhere anymore. He's found himself in a barren and surreal land and there's nothing there at all telling him the way to go.

So Justin and the Compadre have a long heart to heart.

It's not the way that you say it
When you do those things to me.
It's more the way that you mean it
When you tell me what will be.

Justin's wondering about two things: The first is "those things you (the Compadre) do to me" — just what has happened to him so far on the path. And the second is "what will be" — what's waiting for Justin tomorrow and the next day and the next day after that on this path that seems to be endless and, at present, hopeless.

But the Compadre can do nothing about what's happening to Justin; things just have to be gone through. There aren't any shortcuts.

I'm Just Beginning to See

And, as far as "what will be," Justin's completely misunderstanding the Compadre; because "what will be" is, can only be, a mystery.

And when you stop and think about it
You won't believe it's true
That all the love you've been giving
Has all been meant for you.

Maybe Justin thinks the Compadre's playing head games with him. Or maybe Justin thinks the Compadre's intentionally misleading him.

Either way, Justin's convinced that he now needs help, a lot of help, a miracle even, to get him out of this land that he's found himself in in the *Middle Song.*

I'm looking for someone to change my life
I'm looking for a miracle in my life.

It's been tough since that *Tuesday Afternoon* when the journey began.

And if you could see what it's done to me
To lose the love I knew
You'd safely lead me through.

Justin longs for the forever afternoon — that afternoon when the fantastic spell was first cast. That *Tuesday Afternoon* when he felt something more far-reaching (and more inescapable) than he ever imagined

59

possible. *That's* where he wants the Compadre to "lead" him through to — to lead him *back* to.

For the fact is, it's not only the path *ahead* that's calling to Justin now, but it's the path *behind* that's calling to him, too.

Between the silence of the mountains
And the crashing of the sea
There lies a land I once lived in
And she's waiting there for me.

Ron and Maggie Tear

The barren and surreal landscape of The Middle Song.

Back *there* is the Fairyland of Love. And back *there* is the Garden of the Goddess and the Blue Onyx on the Sea. But going back *there* is just not possible — because there *is* no going back — ever.

Justin needs to get the idea of "a land I once lived in" out of his head; he needs to turn his head and heart in the only direction there is in Life.

But in the grey of the morning
My mind becomes confused
Between the dead and the sleeping
And the road that I must choose.

Justin can't see through the mist. He can't see the path at all. There's nothing *here* in this desolate land he's found himself in. Only the silence of an eerie void. *Here* there's only "the dead and the sleeping."
He really can't get any more lost than he is now.

I'm looking for someone to change my life
I'm looking for a miracle in my life.

And if you could see
What it's done to me
To lose the love I knew
You'd safely lead me to
The land that I once knew
To learn as we grow old
The secrets of our soul.

Even so, Justin's original purpose, expressed in *Tuesday Afternoon,* "I've got to find out why," hasn't changed here in *The Middle Song*: "To learn as we grow old, the secrets of our soul." Self discovery.

Song Fourteen — It's Up to You

"We either make ourselves miserable,
or we make ourselves strong.
The amount of work is the same."
—Carlos Castaneda

In *It's Up to You* it's the Compadre's turn to have *his* say in the heart to heart in Justin's head. It's Autumn, the leaves are falling, and the time has come for Justin to realize something very important.

When the breeze between us calls,
Love comes and lingers into our lives.
And the leaves begin to fall,
You point your finger at me.
I love you, I love you.

It's the Compadre, pointing his finger right at Justin: "Justin, you keep looking at me — for *me* to do something. Your sadness saddens me and I love you and I'll always be with you but ..."

In the sadness of your smile
Love is an island way out to sea.
But it seems so long ago
We have been ready trying to be free.

"... love is *not* an island way out to sea. It's much closer than you think. You ..."

And it's up to you
Why won't you say?

"... must roll up your sleeves and realize that *it's up to you.* Stop looking for miracles in your life!"

Make our lives turn out this way.

And, "Our Fate is in *your* hands," is how the Compadre sums it all up to Justin.

Then, with the Compadre's 'tough love' words still in his head, Justin gets his mettle back.

If they knew that we have got nothing to lose
No reason to hide from what's true.

"Nothing to lose!" How *meaningful* these words are. "Nothing to lose." It's a special moment. And, "no reason to hide from what's true." Yes. A thousand times, yes.

Justin has found his way again. (Of course, he was *always* on his way.)

In the world of me and you
All is forgotten when we're inside.
And the words that pass us by
I'm not listening, all of its lies.

When Justin and the Compadre are <u>one</u>, the "lies that kill the Light" have no effect at all.

Song Fifteen — Dawning is the Day

Earth, isn't this what you want:
An invisible re-arising in us?
—Rainer Maria Rilke

Things are looking up for Justin in the song *Dawning is the Day* — the Tao Song.

It's a forever morning perhaps. And "dawn is a feeling, a beautiful ceiling" wrote Justin Hayward's own true sempai, Mike Pinder, who brought Justin Hayward on board The Moody Blues and who helped create the sounds of the songs in this story. I've been writing here only about the lyrics and the meanings that I've found in the lyrics in *I'm Just Beginning to See*. But, just as the unconscious is a land of no-words, so music, too, is a land of no-words itself. And I know that like me, you, too, have found just as much meaning in the music of Justin Hayward's songs as you have found in the words of Justin Hayward's songs. And you've probably also realized that the sum of the lyric and the music, when put together in a song, somehow add up to more than was there separately.

OK. Let's get back on track, shall we.

In *Dawning is the Day* all the gentle voices of Nature are trying to reconnect with Justin — to get him headed in the right direction again.

Rise, let us see you
Dawning is the day.

Miss, misty meadow
You will find your way.

The gentle voices, Nature, telling Justin a new day has dawned and that he needs to think back now and try to recall the Beginning, that very special afternoon, when nothing mattered at all.

Wake up in the morning to yourself
And leave this crazy life behind you.
Listen, we're trying to find you.

Nature's also telling Justin that it's time for him to put the (seemingly) "crazy" events he's experienced on the path up to now "behind" him; because Justin's gone as deeply as he can go within himself and it's time now for him to start seeking in new directions. And Nature starts to *find* Justin: "listen we're trying to find you." And the wondrous thing about this is that as Nature starts to find Justin again, Justin, who left himself behind in *Tuesday Afternoon*, starts to find *himself* again. Because they are one and the same thing — Nature finding Justin *is* Justin finding Nature.

The Gentle Voices of nature then have this simple message for Justin:

Flow to the sea
You know where to go.
Still we are free
No one tells the wind which way to blow.

Look at the river. How much effort is it making in its journey to the sea? None at all. And the wind, too. It just blows freely. The gentle voices are saying: "It's *easy*, Justin. All this while you have been thinking how hard it is. This path. This quest. This search. And all this while you've been wrong. It's easy. It's not difficult. It's Tao. It's easy." And *that's* the key.

Tao is merely a question of balance.

Wake up in the morning to yourself
Open your eyes and start to be you.
Listen, we think we can see you.

The trees are drawing Justin near again. And all the powers of Nature, the true powers of the Earth, are again calling to Justin and they're telling him this: "start to be you." It's a call to Enlightenment.

Baby there's no price upon your head,
Sing it, shout it.

A shooting star-like moment: "*Sing it*" and *"Shout it."* There's "nothing to lose." Nothing.

Now the angry words have all been said,
Do it don't doubt it.

Justin must trust everything that has happened to him. And, likewise, Justin must not doubt that that he has to do.

Wake up in the morning to yourself
Open your head and look around you.

Look! Look and See! There's only one real teacher and it's all around you. Earth.

Listen we think we have found you
Listen we think we can see you.

The Bluebird and the Nightingale, Guinevere and Merlin, the Gypsy who just wants to go Home and the Burrowing Mole who just want to find the Sunlight, the Silent Mountains and the Crashing Sea and the Sky, the Sun, the Moon and the Stars are now all spiraling into alignment for Justin.

Sixth LP — Every Good Boy Deserves Favour

In which a destiny is realized and a home is left forever behind.

Song Sixteen — The Story in Your Eyes

Your fate loves you. One day it will
be entirely yours. Just as you dream
it. If you remain constant to it.
—Frau Eva to Emil Sinclair in *Demian*

Fate. "Just what you want to be/you will be in the end."

Fortune. "What the seeds of her thoughts/wants me to be."

In the movie *Bagger Vance*, Bagger Vance, the caddy who appeared out of nowhere one day, was trying to get the washed up golfer Rannulph Junah ready for a big match against Bobby Jones and Walter Hagen — the two greatest golfers of their time. Then, just when Rannulph Junah was about to give up and drop out of the match, Bagger Vance said this to him: "Inside each and every one of us is one true authentic swing. Something we was born with. Something that is ours and ours alone. I'm right here with ya. I've been here *all along*. Now play the game. Your game. The one that was given to you when you come into this world."

In *The Story in Your Eyes,* Justin realizes his "one true authentic swing"— songwriting.

I've been thinking 'bout our fortune.
And I've decided that we're really not to blame

Our fortune." Fate — Justin's and the Compadre's.
And there's no one to "blame" for Fate.

For the love that's deep inside us now
Is still the same.

And the end of all our exploring
Will be to arrive where we started
And to know the place for the first time.
—T. S. Eliot

Then, a new and very last "reflection" of <u>they</u> that are sleeping inside appears.

And the sound we make together
Is the music to the story in your eyes.
It's been shining down upon me now
I realize.

Justin finds the Songwriter. ("I've been here *all along*," Bagger Vance said.) It's the words and it's the music, together now, making the song. It's the song-writer (Justin) putting music to the story that was there in the Goddess's eyes all along. It's the key that's going to open the door.

Now Justin understands his *very own* story more than ever. Now Justin's Fate is very close.

Listen to the tide slowly turning
Wash all our heartaches away.

Something new is now heard in the "sound of the sea." And it's transforming Justin. All the hard tacks and pain, all the disappointment and confusion, are being washed away.

We're part of the fire that is burning
And from the ashes we can build to another day.

And there's the Phoenix, rising out of *his* pyre that *he* himself built for his *own* rebirth.

But then, without any warning at all, Justin expresses a real and deep uncertainty about everything.

But I'm frightened for your children
That the life that we are living is in vain
And the sunshine we've been waiting for
Will turn to rain.

Justin sings about the "children" again — just like he did in *Hundred* and *Million*. And, in these few lines of lyrics, Justin's very private journey on the path has embraced all mankind. Justin knows he's very close now (he feels it deeply). And it's got him spooked a little. So close to something so meaningful. He's taking the weight of the world onto his shoulders. It's a shared fortune. ("We are all we've got.") You and me. It all just *can't* end in a <u>wasteland</u>, can it?

And then, the final verse:

When the final line is over
And it's certain that the curtain's gonna fall
I can hide inside your sweet, sweet love
Forevermore.

When the final lyric of Justin's final song is written and recorded and sung, Justin knows that he'll be in the arms of _____...

...I'm going to leave this one word in the story in the songs blank, I think. There are many words that could go here (for me, *the Mystery* would do) but whether or not any of them are correct, I can not say. So, Reader of this book, I'm going to leave this one little piece of the story entirely up to you.

"Now play the game, your game, the
one that only you was meant to play."

71

Another Break—Home/The Other Side of Life

Home — straight lines leading to a known future, a sanctuary, a safe harbourage.

And then — the *Other* World.

The Other Side of Life — mystery, doubt, "uncharted seas," and an entirely different language. (The language of this story in the songs, in fact.)

In the context of our story, we can roughly call Home, <u>turning around and going back</u>, and the *Other Side of Life*, <u>going forward</u>.

But nothing will happen in the direction of home — going back to the known. And all that *can* happen is only in the direction that takes us to the other side of life — going forward into the fantastic *unknown*.

We must do what Emil Sinclair says in *Demian*: "All of the moments of calm, the islands of peace that I felt, the islands of magic, I leave behind in the enchanted distance. Nor do I ask to ever set foot there again."

The enchanted past. The "land I once lived in."

And Emil Sinclair also says this: "the impulses always came from the 'other world.'" Because it's only the other side of life that will set you free. And it's only there that you can "lose your way" and go "completely astray" and "find yourself again." Justin left himself behind on the Forever Afternoon; now the time has come for Justin to find himself again.

The time has come for Justin to break with the past. To break with the past! Nothing can happen unless we do! It's the biggest step along the way.

I referenced the J. H. songs
The Other Side of Life and
I Dreamed Last Night.

Song Seventeen — You Can Never Go Home

At the darkest moment comes the light.
—Joseph Campbell

You Can Never Go Home is the Satori Song. A song of the Light. But you wouldn't think so after reading the first verse.

I don't know what I'm searching for
I never have opened the door.
Tomorrow might find me at last
Turning my back on the past.

Right after the hopelessness of the first two lines, though, the germ of an idea, "turning my back on the past," starts to grow in Justin's mind.

But time will tell
Of stars that fell
A million years ago.

The Light from a nova, a fallen star, can take an eon to reach us. (Even at 186,000 miles a second!) And, when we look up into the sky and see it, we're looking at something that happened, started, "a million years ago." But it *has* made its way here. To Earth. For Justin. It was destined to come and it was always going to happen. ("... to transform itself in us.")
To know the secrets of our soul.

74

Memories can never
Take you back
Home
Sweet
Home.

Home. The order and the certainty of childhood.
The realm of plans made and of futures assured. The
well beaten path. The love of the *Tuesday Afternoon.*
"Tuesday's Dead," Cat Stevens sang. Yes, it *is* dead
— and Justin can never go back there again.

You can never go home...

And the moment of seeing is on the next word.

...anymore.

"Anymore." Satori.

All my life I never really knew me 'til today.

The Light.

Now I know why,
I'm just another step along the way.

"I'm just another step along the way." Even in this
amazing moment Justin is wise enough to know that
the path will go on. But things will now never be the

same; from now on, everything on the path will be different.

What follows, then, are four magical couplets that all happen in that single moment of Light.

One:

I lie awake for hours, I'm just waiting for the sun
When the journey we are making has begun.

A new path has started for Justin and his steady and true (and amazing) friend, the Compadre.

Two:

Don't deny the feeling that is stealing through your
    heart
Every happy ending needs to have a start.

No more lies. No more deceit.
The new horizon.

Three:

Weep no more for treasures you've been searching for
   in vain,
'Cos the truth is gently falling with the rain.

It was so easy. Why did Justin have to struggle for
so long? It was like a single leaf falling from a tree and
silently landing in the forest. It was ... after all ... all
explained "with a sigh."

Four:

High above the forest lie the pastures of the sun
Where the two that learned the secret now are one.

Justin and the Compadre are one. Justin and Nature
are one. Justin and his Fate are one.
It was what Justin was seeking all along.

"You'll have to listen within yourself,
then you will notice that I am within
you. Do you understand?"
—Demian's last words to Emil Sinclair.

Seventh LP — Seventh Sojourn
In which a new path is started.

Song Eighteen — New Horizons

Looking up, blue sky over me
There's a soft grass 'tween my toes
A gentle spring wind blows.
—Livingston Taylor

I said in the introduction that I knew very little about Justin Hayward's personal life. But I *do* happen to know that, at the time *Seventh Sojourn* came out, Justin Hayward was married and had a young daughter. And so, in the first verse of the song *New Horizons*, when Justin sings that he has "love enough for three," it's his small family that he's singing about.

New Horizons finds the Justin in our story in the songs, though, walking a new path — a path with heart.

There I travel, and the only worthwhile challenge is to traverse its full length—looking, looking breathlessly.
        —Don Juan, the Yaqui desert-walker.

Justin's back. But, he won't ever be all the way back; that will never happen. Because no one ever fully gets back from the special kind of experience that Justin's had. The artist will always, until the day he or she dies, carry it inside. And though the road *was* often confusing and painful it was, also, the greatest adventure.

78

Justin's new horizon — the "gentler path."

Well I've had dreams enough for one
And I've got love enough for three.
I have my hopes to comfort me
I got my new horizons out to sea.

But I'm never going to lose
Your precious gift
It will always be that way.

"I'm never going to lose your precious gift." Well,
in *my* version of the story, I believe Justin's talking to
his Compadre — his dear Compadre.

'Cos I know I'm gonna find
My own peace of mind
Some day.

Justin knows that a deeper peace of mind still awaits
him — some day.

Where is this place that we have found.

Earth!

Nobody knows where we are bound.

The "uncharted sea!"

And, then, the past is remembered.

I long to hear, I need to see
'Cos I've shed tears too many for me.

But *now* everything's changed.

On the wind,
Soaring free
Spread your wings
I'm beginning to see.

On *Tuesday Afternoon*, at the start of the journey, Justin sang, "I'm <u>just</u> beginning to see." Here, on *New Horizons*, he sings, "I'm beginning to see." Only the <u>just</u> is gone. But losing this <u>just</u> has meant a lot — it has brought Justin his freedom.

Out of mind
Far from view
Beyond the reach of
The nightmare come true.

The "tormented soul" is now and forever a thing of the past.

Song Nineteen — You and Me
co-written with Graeme Edge

The mockingbird sings each different song;
Each song has wings, they won't stay long.
—Richie Havens' *Follow*

I suspect that this song's music was written by Justin Hayward and its lyric was written by Graeme Edge.

You and Me is the Concert Song. In it, Justin is doing just what he wants to do — sing his songs and play his guitar for those of us who want to listen.

You and Me: Vietnam, the Middle East, religion, things environmental, the Moodies and their fans. That is the gist of this song.

But this song contains two splendid lines — two lines that hold about one thousand lines worth of wisdom.

All we are trying to say
Is that we are all we've got.

"We are all we've got." We are the answer. The only answer. To everything. Walt Kelly gave *these* word's for Pogo to say: "We have met the enemy and he is us." It's the same thing. We are the answer. So ... when will we ever learn? When will we *ever* learn?

There's a leafless tree in Asia / Under the sun there's a homeless man. / There's a forest fire in the valley / Where the story all began. / What will be our last thought / Do you think it's coming soon. / Will it be of comfort / Or the pain of a burning wound? / All we are trying to say is / We are all we've got. / You and me just cannot fail / If we never, never stop. / You're an ocean full of faces / And you know that we believe / We're just a wave that drifts around you /Singing all our hopes and dreams. / We look around in wonder /At the work that has been done / By the visions of our father / Touched by his loving son.

**The Filmore East West
1968–1969
The Moody Blues
in concert
Chicago Transit Authority
Jethro Tull * Richie Havens**

Song Twenty — The Land Of Make-Believe

Whilst all the stars that round her burn,
And all the planets in their turn,
Confirm the tidings as they roll,
And spread the truth from pole to pole.
—Joseph Addison

In *The Land of Make-Believe*, the last song in the story, Justin's now a teacher. He can't walk the path for anyone else, but he *can* sing the truth of what he has learned on the road *he* has traveled.

We're living in a land of make-believe
And trying not to let it show.
Maybe in that land of make-believe
Heartaches can turn into joy.

Justin's no longer singing "I" and "me" and "my;" he's now singing "we" and "us" and "our." And it's not about himself and the Compadre anymore; it's about himself and *us* now.

The first verse of the song is about the world inside — the "land of make-believe." It's Justin's secret world that he tries not to "show" to anyone. (Except, of course, when millions of copies of Moody Blues LPs are sold and listened to.)

And this "land of make-believe" — where the story in the songs took place — is where Justin's "heart-aches ... turn into joy."

Next, the world outside.

We're breathing in the smoke of high and low.
We're taking up a lot of room
Somewhere in the dark and silent night
    /lonely night
Our prayer will be heard, make it soon.

The "smoke of high," truth, "and low," thoughts they cannot defend. And then, here in the last song, Justin Hayward gives us one last mystery: a "prayer." But it's *our* prayer; it's there in each and every one of us. So ... you *know* what this prayer is.

And, then, it's Justin's first lesson. And it's Nature, of course, that's going to deliver it.

So fly little bird/Up into the clear blue sky

Alasdair Mitchell

And carry the word/Love's the only reason why.

84

And the very end of the story *is* Justin's first lesson:

Open all the shutters on your windows
Unlock all the locks upon your doors
Brush away the cobwebs from your daydreams
No secrets come between us anymore.
Oh say it's true
Only love can see you through
You know what love can do to you.

All you need to do is to "open" and to "unlock" and to "brush away" and to find the secret of yourself. The something inside that is yours and yours alone — the something inside that is you and you alone.

The End.

Afoot and light-hearted I take to the open road,
Healthy, free, the world before me,
The long brown path before me leading wherever
    I choose.

Henceforth I ask not good-fortune,
I myself am good-fortune.

Seven Conclusions

1. See!

My mind is back behind my eyes
And there before me sits a butterfly.
—Justin Hayward

To catch all that there is we *must* see and we *must* listen with both sets of our senses — those of our conscious mind and those of our unconscious mind.

The clouds in the sky, the rocks along the shore, and the trees in the forest — they all want us to *look* at them. And they all want us to *listen* to them. As does all Nature. (As does the Mystery.)

And to hear the sun, what a thing to believe
But it's all around if we could but perceive.
—Graeme Edge

We are the cosmos experiencing itself in ways the cosmos never before could and in ways that it never will again. The intersection of everything is there in our very senses.

In us, the most fleeting of all.
Just once, everything, only
for once. And never again.
(Only here! On Earth!)
—Rainer Maria Rilke

2. The Land of No-Words.

There is inside us a land of no-words, the unconscious. And it's our ability to venture into this land, and there to find ourselves, that makes us human. For many, this land is quickly conquered by religion. For others, this land inside is just ignored. But for the seeker, like the Justin in this story, the unconscious is not programmable and not ignored. The seeker is left entirely to his or her own wits to make some rhyme and reason of it all — "to find out why." And the seeker's only help are the sign posts and clues left by other seekers in novels and poems, in songs and in pictures, and in rare encounters with <u>teachers</u>.

3. Art.

It is the <u>artist</u> that's most likely to lead us any place of worth in this crazy world; they are the true heroes of the human heart. The artist, no matter how ridiculous he or she sometimes appears, is probably a thousand times more capable at running things than is *any* statesman.

People are *always* scrutinizing religion and science. And they are *always* forgetting art. Religion and science don't seem to understand what Art is all about.

He (the artist) is responsible for humanity, for animals even. He will have to make his inventions smelt, touched, heard. —Arthur Rimbaud

And there's Vincent, waking up early and then off to the countryside around Arles to paint. (Did he even have enough money for a breakfast?) And, as he walks along a narrow road between two *blazing* fields, he is overwhelmed by all that he "sees." It's all there in the morning air and in the birds darting. It's all there in the sounds of the earth that he hears and in the swelling waves of wheat that are around him. And it's all too much for him to take in — he's touched to the core by something indescribable. And his only thoughts are that he must, *somehow*, communicate all of this in his painting today. He must, *somehow*, find the right colors to show that he's understood God today.

"Look out on a summer's day with eyes
that know the darkness in my soul."

89

4. The Light is not Supernatural.

If on this one single point the whole human race could get its head straight, what a better chance there would be for this tiny speck of sand in this almost infinite cosmos of 100 billion galaxies.

It's so simple. Just do away with the supernatural. For good.

Imagine nothing supernatural;
It's easy if you try.

5. The Rebel.

Though there had been rebels writing songs of rebellion for centuries, the number of songs they wrote weren't that many and the ideas in their songs they wrote were mostly about fighting real rebellions. But, in the 1930's, Woody Guthrie started a new ball rolling. Woody's songs back then were deeper and more poetic than anything before and they started to stretch the boundaries of what a song was all about.

The underground current of rebellious song-writing grew in the 1940's and the 1950's. And then, in the 1960's, an explosion. What happened in the 1960's was honestly amazing. Music that was unimaginable before started to be written and to be listened to and to be literally *lived.* And it was there, in that magical-mystery time of the mid-1960's that Justin Hayward arrived on the scene.

But Justin Hayward was not a rebel like most of the other rebels of his time. While they were writing songs against war and against conformity and against big business, Justin Hayward was taking his songs in a very different direction.

Justin Hayward was a rebel in the same way that the poets Arthur Rimbaud and Gerald Manley Hopkins were; Justin Hayward was a rebel of the human spirit. (Which is why Justin Hayward's songs are so secretive and kind of ... coded.)

6. Trust.

We have to trust all the <u>events</u> and all the encounters in our lives—the good *and* the bad. They all guide us in the direction that we were meant to go. We have to forgive the past and we have to forget the past.

We have to trust our Intuition and our Instinct. They are "a far better guide in the long run than our Intellect," Henry Miller said.

And finally, we have to trust in Nature and not live in ways that oppose Nature.

7. These Words, These Days.

As I'm writing these words things are falling apart everywhere in the world. I guess that things are always falling apart or being put together or being put back together. But now it really does seem that we're on the brink of a super devitalized Earth.

So I'm going to end these conclusions with an idea inspired by Justin Hayward's and John Lodge's song *Strange Times* — about the dire straits that the earth is in everywhere.

This *is* what the world was 20,000 years ago:

Long time ago, Back in the mist of time
Back when the crystal waters flowed;
There was a world ; So strange and so beautiful
All life would flourish and would grow.

But now migrating birds and migrating whales are losing their ways, thousands of species of animals are dying, poisons are collecting in the cells of every living thing and in every drop of water and on every square inch of land, glaciers and icecaps are melting, oceans, the heart and soul of the earth, are losing their vitality, *paradises are being paved and parking lots are being put up*, and what are we doing, we who are responsible for all of this.

There *is* a world
So warped and so brutalized.

"Don't let Terra die," Justin Hayward would sing. The Forever Afternoons will all disappear and any hope of us ever finding ourselves will also disappear <u>if we don't listen to the voices of Nature that are desperately calling to us now</u>.

Justin Hayward & The Moody Blues in Context

1. In Context.

There isn't anything in this world that can be known well without context. Because leaving out context leaves only the fundamental.

Without context things down in the depths of Justin Hayward's songs, and their <u>coded mysteries</u>, will go unnoticed. And, without any context, all the stuff that the Moody Blues' songs are made of might slip by.

I'm not trying to beat my readers over the head with the profound. I'm just saying that connecting things creates a kind of harmonic understanding. This is all that I tried to do in *I'm Just Beginning to See*.

2. Frames of Reference in the Moody Blues.

Mike Pinder wrote:

"*Everything's turning, turning around*"
–Sun is Still Shining

It's <u>astronomy</u> and it's the <u>Tao</u> story of the Music of Heaven. Nothing in the entire cosmos isn't moving. It's all turning — revolving or rotating or expanding. The Native American <u>Black Elk</u> said this: "Everything the power of the world does, is done in a circle. The Sky is round and I have heard that the Earth is round like a ball. The Sun comes and goes down again in a circle."

Ray Thomas wrote:

"Wasn't where I should have been" ...
So I went out and strolled about looking at the shops.
Didn't see anything I liked
So I didn't buy anything.
 —Dear Diary

It's a kind of droll <u>existentialism</u> — Ray Thomas cleverly telling us that he's feeling a little out of place in this world that he's found himself in. He wants and needs to buy something, to give it all some meaning, but there's just nothing out there for him *to* buy on the store shelves and in the show windows of life.

John Lodge wrote:

I worked like a slave for years
Sweat so hard just to end my fears
Not to end my life a poor man
But by now I know I should have run.
 —Ride My Seesaw

It's a theme throughout <u>English literature</u> — we're given just one chance at life so be sure that you get it right as soon as you can: "When I was one-and- twenty / I heard a wise man say / Give crowns and pounds and guineas / But not your heart away." John Lodge, like A. E. Houseman's *Shropshire Lad*, is discovering that "time cannot be won."

94

Graeme Edge wrote:

And he saw the tree above him, and the stars,
And the veins in the leaf, and the light,
And the balance, and he saw a magnificent perfection.
    —The Balance

The Earth, today, is way more out of balance than when Graeme Edge wrote these words in 1970. And I think that in a few decades it's going to be so out of whack that there'll be a lot of catastrophes. Environmentalism will then, maybe just maybe, start to be understood. Will the "there-are-no-environmental problems" people continue to laugh at and to make fun of the wildlife lovers and those raising the alarm 50 years from now. (My depressed guess is, "yes.")

Context and frames of reference in poetry and in paintings, in environmentalism and in enlightenment, in music and myth, in comparative religion and in chaos theory, in reptiles crawling over hot sands and in crustaceans clambering over sandy sea floors, in philosophy and in psychology, in Van Gogh's spirals and in a seeker's heart on a lonely desert trail. Connecting everything. Meanings in birds and in botany, in aliens from space and in archaeology, in creation and in evolution, in the ancient and in a future history, in God in no-god in all the Greek and Norse and Thai Gods, in the transcendental and in the intuitive. It all rings true. It all calls out.

3. A Path Explained

In 1972 I was lucky enough to attend a talk by Paul Reps in Boulder, Colorado. In his book *Zen Bones, Zen Flesh,* there's a Zen version of the "steps along the way."

The 10 Bulls
by Kakuan in the 12th century

The bull is the eternal principle of life — truth in action. The ten bulls represent the sequence of steps in the realization of one's true nature. An understanding of the creative principle of the 10 Bulls transcends any time or place. The 10 Bulls is a revelation of human experience.

One — The Search for the Bull   "In the pasture of this world, I endlessly push aside the tall grasses in search of the bull."

Two — Discovering the Footprints "Along the riverbank under the trees, I discover footprints! How will I perceive the true from the untrue?"

Three — Perceiving the Bull   "I hear the song of the nightingale. The sun is warm, the wind is mild, and willows are green along the shore. Here no bull can hide!"

<u>Four — Catching the Bull</u> "I seize him with a terrific struggle. His great will and power are inexhaustible. He charges to the high plateau far above the cloud-mists."

<u>Five — Taming the Bull</u> "The whip and rope are necessary else he might stray off down some dusty road. Being well trained, he becomes naturally gentle. Then, unfettered, he obeys his master."

<u>Six — Riding the Bull Home</u> "Mounting the bull, slowly I return homeward. The voice of my flute intones through the evening."

<u>Seven — The Bull Transcended</u> "Astride the bull, I reach home. I am serene. The bull too can rest. Within my thatched dwelling I have abandoned the whip and rope."

<u>Eight — Both Bull and Self Transcended</u> "Whip, rope, person, and bull — all merge in No-Thing. How may a snowflake exist in a raging fire?"

<u>Nine — Reaching the Source</u> "The water *is* emerald, the mountain *is* indigo, and I see that which is creating and that which is destroying."

<u>Ten — In the World</u> "Barefooted, I mingle with the people of the world. Nobody knows me and there before me the dead trees become alive."

4. The 1970 Bantam Cover for *Demian.*

5. The Singular Fellowship.

A few of the adventurers guilty of giving context to this book.

Hermann Hesse — was a German writer (1877–1962). He volunteered to fight in WWI but soon saw the insanity of it all and wrote an essay warning people not to fall for nationalism. For this, he had to flee Germany. He settled and lived the second half of his life secluded in the mountains in Switzerland.

Carl Jung — was a Swiss psychologist (1875-1961). He scientifically studied and found deep new meanings in that part of us we call our "soul." And he explored possibly every expression of that wordless land: astrology, dream analysis, sociology, philosophy, religion, Gnosticism, synchronicity! and symbolism.

Gerald Manley Hopkins — was an English poet and Jesuit priest (1844-1889). Though he endured terrible melancholy, he was an innovative poet and invented sprung rhythm! He connected God and Nature.

Glory be to God for dappled things—
For skies of couple-colour as a brinded cow;
For rose-moles all in stipple upon trout that swim;
Fresh-firecoal chestnut-falls; finches' wings;
Landscape plotted and pieced—fold, fallow, and plow.
  —Pied Beauty

Joseph Campbell — was an American mythologist (1904-1987). He was an unknown academic until he burst into the hearts and heads of many people worldwide after his **PBS TV** special, *The Power of Myth,* explained the importance of the Myth that lies deep down in our psyches.

Chet Raymo — is an American enlightened scientist and writer (1936). His stunning, heartrending novel *In the Falcon's Claw* lays out Europe's tug-of-war between Naturalism and Supernaturalism in the year 1000. I was very, very lucky to discover this amazing writer.

Walt Whitman — was an American poet and humanist (1819-1892). Every American, if they want to understand what America was, *is, supposed* to be about, needs to read, from cover to cover, *Leaves of Grass.* There's no word to define his poetry, though *ecstatic* is often used.

Cat Stevens — is/was/is an English (Greek father/Swedish mother) singer-songwriter (1948). A true songwriting rebel of the human spirit in the early 70's. Then, after a perplexing (to me) change of heart in 1979, he put his guitar down and abandoned the path that he was on for another, more paved, path.

Henry Miller — was an American writer (1891-1980). He miserably walked the streets of New York his first 40 years while inside an explosive force was growing bigger and bigger. He finally couldn't bear it anymore. He went to Paris in 1930, wrote two books, and changed what literature was all about.

Carlos Castaneda — was a super reclusive American writer and student of the Yaqui desert-walker Don Juan (1925-1998). He wrote about *separate* realities. He found these new realities, partly, while eating hallucinogenic plants in Southwest America and Mexico.

Rainer Maria Rilke — was an Austrian seeker, poet and writer (1875-1926). I have never read a poet who could put so much meaning into so few words:

"Perhaps all the dragons of our lives
are princesses who are only waiting
to see us once brave and beautiful."

Miguel Serrano — Chilean writer (1917-2009). His meetings and correspondence with Hesse and Jung in Switzerland at the end of their lives is an important, vital, record of those two great men. However, his personal ideas which were very sincere and idealist when he was young, became very strange later in life.

Sylvia Plath — was an American poet (1932-1963) who had a special talent. All she had to do was to walk down a lane in the English countryside and describe what she saw around her — and in these descriptions she revealed to us the deepest parts of her soul.

Paul Reps—was an American zen student, master, artist, haiku poet, and world traveller (1895-1990).

Livingston Taylor — is an American eclectic singer and songwriter (1950). (He has a more famous brother.) His first album has songs on it that are just as strong a memory of 1970 for me as are the songs of Justin Hayward. Many of Livingston Taylor's songs have this an amazing theme — wisdom through "deep kindness."

Vincent van Gogh — was a Dutch painter (1853-1890). A lot of people have a special affinity for the deeply sad Vincent van Gogh who saw God in every expression of nature. Don McLean did and he captured him perfectly in his song *Vincent*: "This world was never meant / For one as beautiful as you."

Nikos Kazantzakis — was a Greek writer (1883-1957). This world needs Nikos Kazantzakis. This world needs a Nikos Kazantzakis heart transplant.

Linda Lewis — is an English (Jamaican father/ English mother) singer/songwriter (1950). A magical voice, she has a five octave vocal range that can send shivers through me when the words are *just right*. Linda Lewis gave me a lot of important yin to balance Justin Hayward's yang.

6. No-Words.

Words are really a mask. They
rarely express the true meaning;
in fact they tend to hide the truth.
— Hermann Hesse

I'm including in this "a little revised" last edition of *I'm Just Beginning to See* a very nearly complete text of *No-Words* — written by a person unknown to me. I suspect that the writer of No-Words is now dead because it was apparently written by someone who was very sick, in intensive care at a hospital, and who indicated in his words that he was dying.

It is important that this *No-Words* confession be written someplace on paper, because its webpage might disappear at any time from the net. (Though it looks like it's been there for 15 years now.) And it *is* important that people find it. I can only hope that within the limited sphere of those few Justin Hayward fans who read this book that it will become better known.

I found *No-Words* simply by searching "no words" on the internet. No-words was a term that I wanted to use in my book and so I wanted to find out if anybody else had used it in the way that I wanted to use it. I got just one result but that one result that I got literally knocked the wind out of me.

It's deep, well written prose-poetry, religion and philosophy. And it touched me — a lot. Who was this person? What were the circumstances of his 47 years of life? Did he somehow survive the ordeal that he was going through?

I've played the editor for *No-Words* — but only just a little. Some spelling, a little grammar and some punctuation etc.

And ... I'm very happy that it could give some context to *I'm Just Beginning to See.*

No-Words

8/3/97

I feel like a deflated balloon, relieved that I don't have to hold my breath.

In the last two years I have crossed over several times from the land that has words to the land that has no words. It has been hard crossing this boundary, both to and from. (Even this word, *hard,* has a different meaning in the world of word than it has in the world of no-words.) These two places don't seem to comprehend each other. No-words does not have much use for words, and words must stop at the frontier.

Why am I writing this in the land of words? I babble because I'm tired, I'm sad, and I'm scared in the land of words. The space of no-words has no fear. I know it is foolish to throw words at the land of no-words. All it can do is mislead, the world of no-words has no contradiction. The world of words has infinite contradiction.

All my life I have heard of this land of no-words, but until these last two years I could never find the door. I now know why, but I have no words to say why.

So this is my introduction to the world of no-words, a world that I have spent some time in, though time doesn't exist there. This is my chronicle not of the land of no-words but how my journeys across the frontier have changed my world of words, how the two seem to be blending. It is hard, this blending.

(The words I write sometimes just betray and confuse, but I must babble, it is my way of crying, in joy and sorrow.)

When I meet someone in the land of words, we work hard to find common ground to stand on. In no-words there is no ground. But when talking with someone in words, at the same time, we can visit in no-words — through the eyes, and we can accept the unknown that we both share.

Many times it is suffering that opens the the gate to no-words, occasionally joy. Joy or suffering, no matter, the only word for no-words is love, but even that betrays the land of no-words.

All my life I have been running desperately to find me. Like the boy running from his shadow not understanding he can stop and rest in the shade. I have been, in all ways that is me, looking for some insight, some understanding of the mysteries of no-words. What is my existence, body, mind, spirit? Is there purpose or connection with God (another no-word word.)

Driven by the belief that I could achieve, through hard work, an opening within, and a journey within, a way out of this world and a home with no suffering. It's hard to let go, to stop running. I must run to be alive, I can't stop running until I have answers. What a waste the land of no-words has no answers and all questions must be discarded at the border crossing.

Much of what I find in the last breath is the time I've spent in the land of no-words, everything else just doesn't fit.

My purpose of existence is who I am and to find the structure to hold no-words. Forgive me. No-words is an opening to birth and death at every moment.

On the frontier, actually when I was wired up in a hospital's intensive care unit, I understood that I didn't want to be alone crossing over. I didn't know this until then. How important it was that someone in words who knows me hold my hand as I cross to no-words. The physical. But felt with no words in my heart.

So much of my life has been building structures of thought, intellect and beliefs. Carefully building an identity in this world when none of it fits. And the time left over from building these structures of my own reality has been spent defending or modifying them. For 47 years it's kept me very busy, leaving little time.

Touching, with the heart, carries me across. In everything I do, I should also find my heart there, with no words.

Why do I write this? To leave something behind. And it won't fit through the door.

Why do I tell my daughter to clean her room and get a good education. It's not the words.

Ty

7. Out of Context.

I wrote *I'm Just Beginning to See: a Story in the Songs of Justin Hayward* because, one day, I saw the story and just felt that *somebody* had to point it out. I'm not a writer and getting my words right, even in this short book, took some months. (Well, about a year, to tell the truth.) But even if the book's a little awkward in some places, I'm happy that I wrote it, published it, and that some people have bought it.

I know this book isn't every Justin Hayward fan's (and every Moody Blues Fan's) cup of tea. There have been a few slings and arrows. But ... since ...

The real meaning of enlightenment is to gaze with undimmed eyes on all darkness.
— Nikos Kazantzakis

... I'll just keep travelling this road. I will. And I'm still thinking I'll see a sign or that I'll have an intuitive thought, any day maybe, that'll help me to make sense of things. I'm losing my faith in books and such.

So I'll head over to Jizo Pond now to see how the egret that's got a broken wing there's doing. It's been making its living along the edge of the pond for about five months now — wanting to fly but never flying, just running and walking and standing and poking its head into the reeds sometimes to catch a small insect and swallow it. I've become very interested in this bird. I think it's about to teach me something.

108

I'm Just Beginning to See

A Few Notes

1. The picture on page 33 is that of Lillian Gish.

2. The picture of the Compadre on page 42 is actually that of Walt Whitman.

3. The word "dæmon," used on page 45, I shoplifted from Philip Pullman's trilogy *His Dark Materials*. The quote on 48 is that of the mythologist Joseph Campbell.

4. The photo on page 60 is of Great Gable, Cumbria by Ron and Maggie Tear. Thanks R & M.

5. The photo on page 84 is by Alasdair Mitchell. Thanks Alasdair.

6. The quote on page 81 is actually from a song by Jerry Merrick and the quote on page 86 is one of, (who else but), Walt Whitman's.

7. The words at the bottom of page 89 are those of Don Mclean. The quote about "parking lots" on page 92 is from Joni Mitchell. (But you knew that already, didn't you.)

Adam Randolph (his pen name) is an American English teacher and (secret) environmental extremist living in Japan and Hawaii with his wife Machiko and their two orphaned street cats Torajiro and Gracie.

Canterbury Cat's lost topic.

I'm Just Beginning to See

44947750R10065

Made in the USA
Charleston, SC
10 August 2015